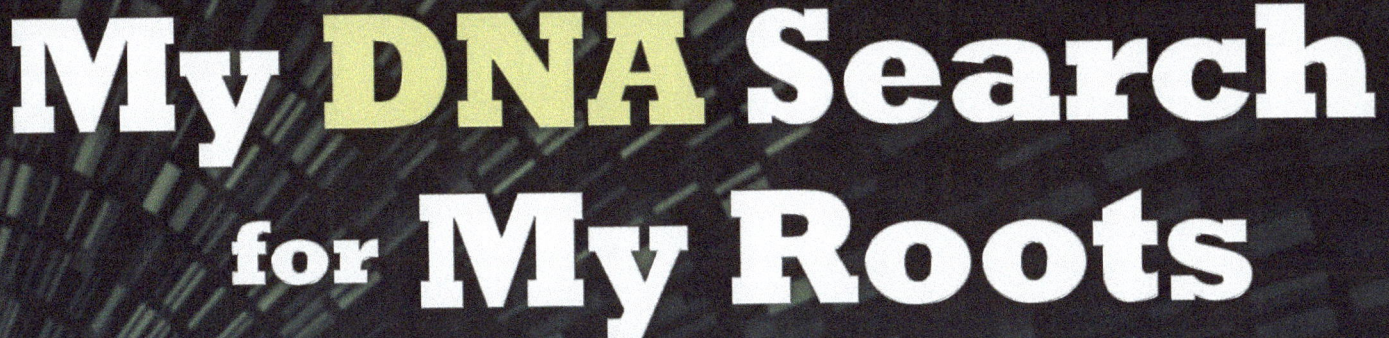

# My DNA Search for My Roots

## Everett Woolum's DNA Journal

by

Everett Woolum

WORKBOOK PRESS LLC
187 E Warm Springs Rd,
Suite B285 Las Vegas NV 89119 USA

Website: https://workbookpress.com/
Hotline: 1-888-818-4856
Email: admin@workbookpress.com


Ordering Information:

Quantity sales. Special discounts are available on quantity purchases by corporations, associations, and others. For details, contact the publisher at the address above.


Library of Congress Control Number:

ISBN-13:        978-1-965732-78-6   Paperback Version


REV. DATE: 07/24/2025

# My DNA Search for My Roots

## Everett Woolum's DNA Journal

by

Everett Woolum

# DEDICATION

For my family and friends.

# ACKNOWLEDGMENTS

A special thank you is in order to my wife, Mary Ann, for being an excellent partner, one that I could always depend upon in any situation, a solid rock in support of our life together. I greatly appreciate the contribution that Brenda, my daughter, for her role in my writing journey.

It is with great pleasure that I acknowledge the significant contribution made by Gustavo   Serra, for his work in editing and for his never-ending encouragement in my effort to complete this project. I am deeply grateful To Dr. Rosita K. Serra for our close friendship through the years while managing rentals, traveling, taking college classes, dancing lessons, going to parties and participating in local activities.

I am indebted to Miss Willow Hopkins for her friendship and for being my excellent realtor for 42 years. I want to thank my mother, father, brothers, sisters and relatives for their help during times of hardships and celebrations. I would not be who I am without you.

This is a separate booklet that describes my 23andMe profile. I hope you'll benefit from reading my life's story through this DNA journal.  This is my legacy that I leave for you.

# 1
## ANCESTRY COMPOSITION

Trace your heritage through the centuries and uncover clues about where your ancestors lived and when.

# 2
## MATERNAL HAPLOGROUP

Learn about the long, unbroken line of women on the maternal side of your family tree.

# 3
## PATERNAL HAPLOGROUP

These are the men of your paternal line. Get to know their story.

# 4
## NEANDERTHAL ANCESTRY

Your DNA may connect you to these extinct humans who interbred with our ancestors long ago.

# 5
## YOUR DNA RELATIVES

Learn insights about your genetic relatives.

# 6

# WHAT CAN SPIT TELL US?

Your spit contains a lot of DNA, packaged tightly inside your cells, which are the building blocks that make up all life on earth. Most of your cells store DNA in two places: in the nucleus and in the mitochondria. It may take a lifetime for you to explore all of the information encoded in your genes, but we hope this book helps you begin your journey.

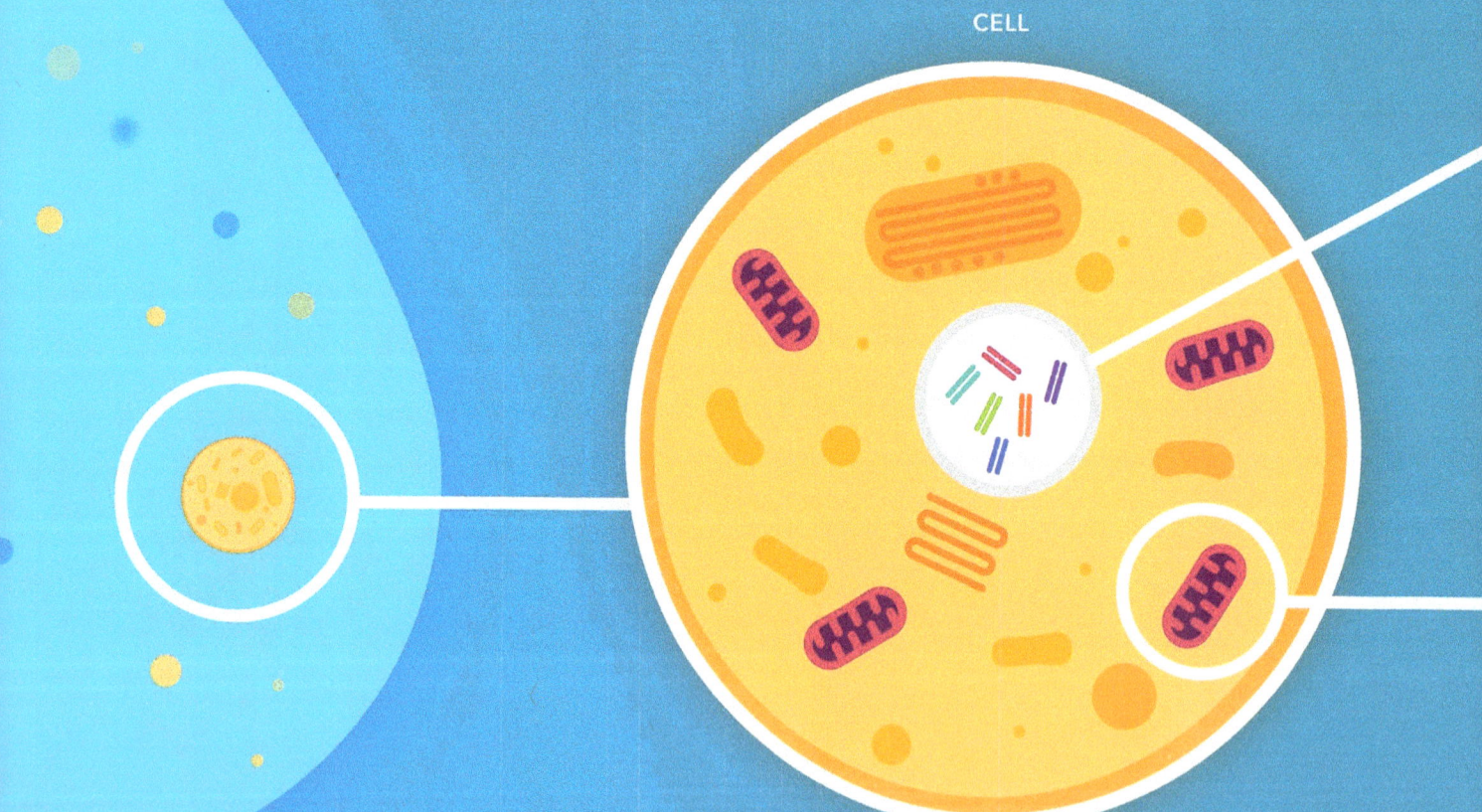

CELL

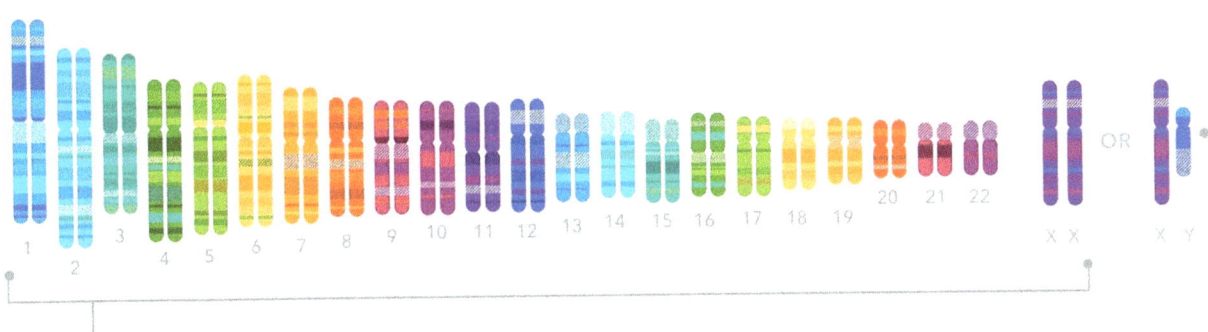

AUTOSOMAL DNA        SEX CHROMOSOMES

1   2   3   4   5   6   7   8   9   10   11   12   13   14   15   16   17   18   19   20   21   22    X X    X Y

**Autosomal and X chromosome DNA**

Autosomes (along with the X sex chromosome) help us determine your Ancestry Composition and Neanderthal Ancestry.

**Y chromosome DNA**

The Y chromosome is one of two sex chromosomes, and has a gene that determines male sex. Paternal haplogroups are traced through genetic variants in the Y chromosome, which females do not inherit.

MITOCHONDRIA

MITOCHONDRIAL DNA

Maternal haplogroups are determined by sets of genetic variants in a tiny, unusual loop of DNA called mitochondrial DNA (mtDNA). As the name suggests, mtDNA is found in mitochondria – small but mighty structures inside our cells that turn fuel from the food we eat into energy.

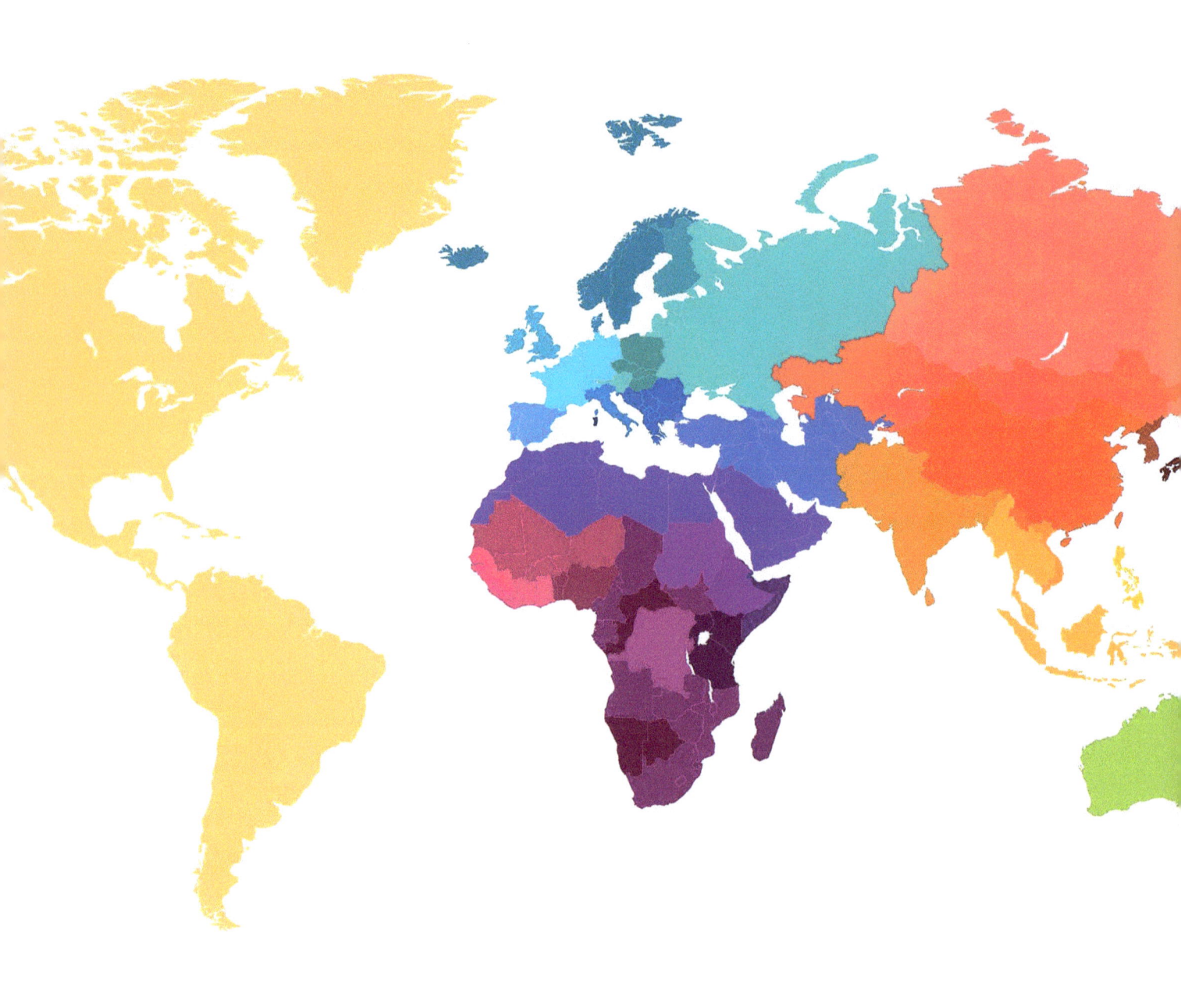

# ANCESTRY COMPOSITION

Your DNA can reveal a lot about your ancestry — where your ancestors may have come from, when and where they may have migrated around the globe, and how you're connected to populations around the world.

# ANCESTRY COMPOSITION

We compare your DNA to that of different populations around the world. When your DNA closely matches the DNA from one of these populations, we assign that ancestry to the corresponding piece of your DNA. Sometimes, DNA resembles reference DNA from several populations, so we assign a "broad" ancestry. The adjacent chart shows a breakdown of where your DNA comes from around the world.

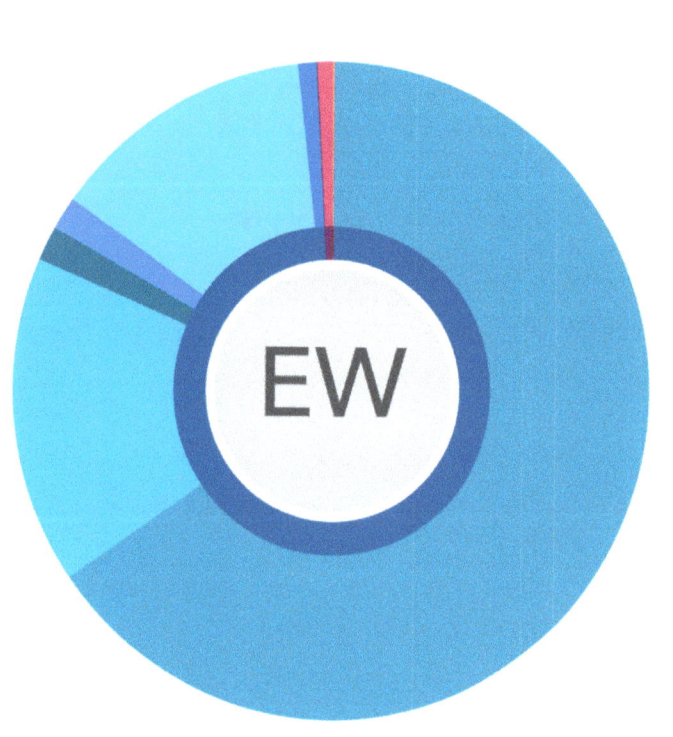

| Everett Woolum | 100% |
|---|---|
| **European** | **99.1%** |
| ● British & Irish<br>United Kingdom, Ireland | 65.3% |
| ● French & German<br>Switzerland, Germany | 16.1% |
| ● Scandinavian | 1.7% |
| ● Spanish & Portuguese | 1.6% |
| ● Broadly Northwestern European | 13.4% |
| ● Broadly Southern European | 0.9% |
| ● Broadly European | 0.1% |
| **Sub-Saharan African** | **0.8%** |
| ● Ghanaian, Liberian & Sierra Leonean | 0.8% |
| **East Asian & Native American** | **0.1%** |
| ● Broadly Northern Asian & Native American | 0.1% |

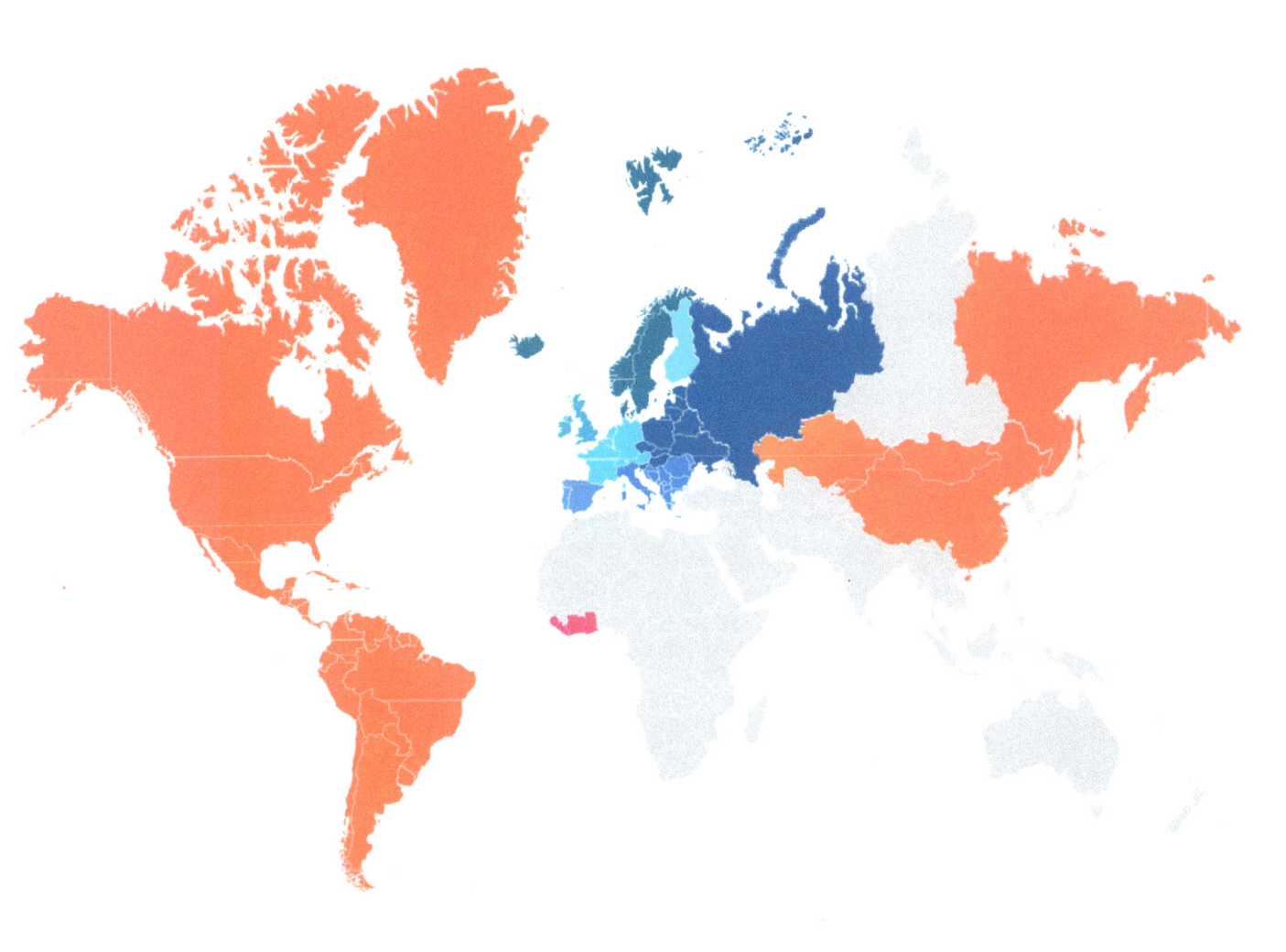

# ANCESTRY TIMELINE

Your Ancestry Timeline is a visual estimation of how many generations ago you may have had an ancestor who descended from a single population. These results may be helpful for learning about your genealogy and for piecing together the history of your ancestors' migrations.

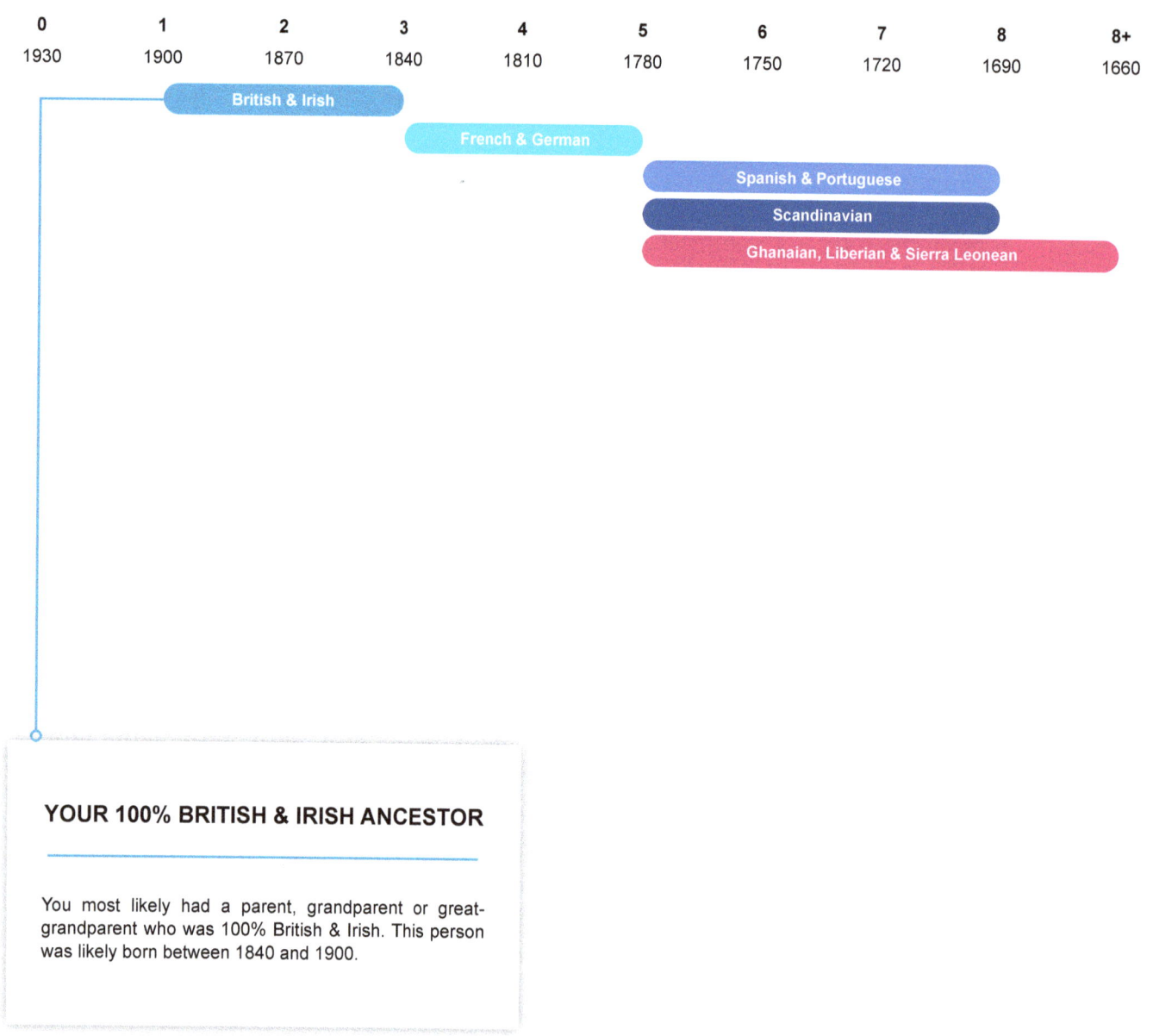

| 0 | 1 | 2 | 3 | 4 | 5 | 6 | 7 | 8 | 8+ |
|---|---|---|---|---|---|---|---|---|---|
| 1930 | 1900 | 1870 | 1840 | 1810 | 1780 | 1750 | 1720 | 1690 | 1660 |

British & Irish

French & German

Spanish & Portuguese

Scandinavian

Ghanaian, Liberian & Sierra Leonean

## YOUR 100% BRITISH & IRISH ANCESTOR

You most likely had a parent, grandparent or great-grandparent who was 100% British & Irish. This person was likely born between 1840 and 1900.

**BRITISH & IRISH**

Lighthouse in Fanad Heath,
Northern Ireland.

# ANCESTRY CHROMOSOME PAINTING

Your Ancestry Chromosome Painting shows how the DNA that matches each specific ancestry is distributed across your chromosomes. Typically, longer pieces of DNA from a particular population suggest a recent ancestor from that population, while shorter pieces suggest a more distant ancestor.

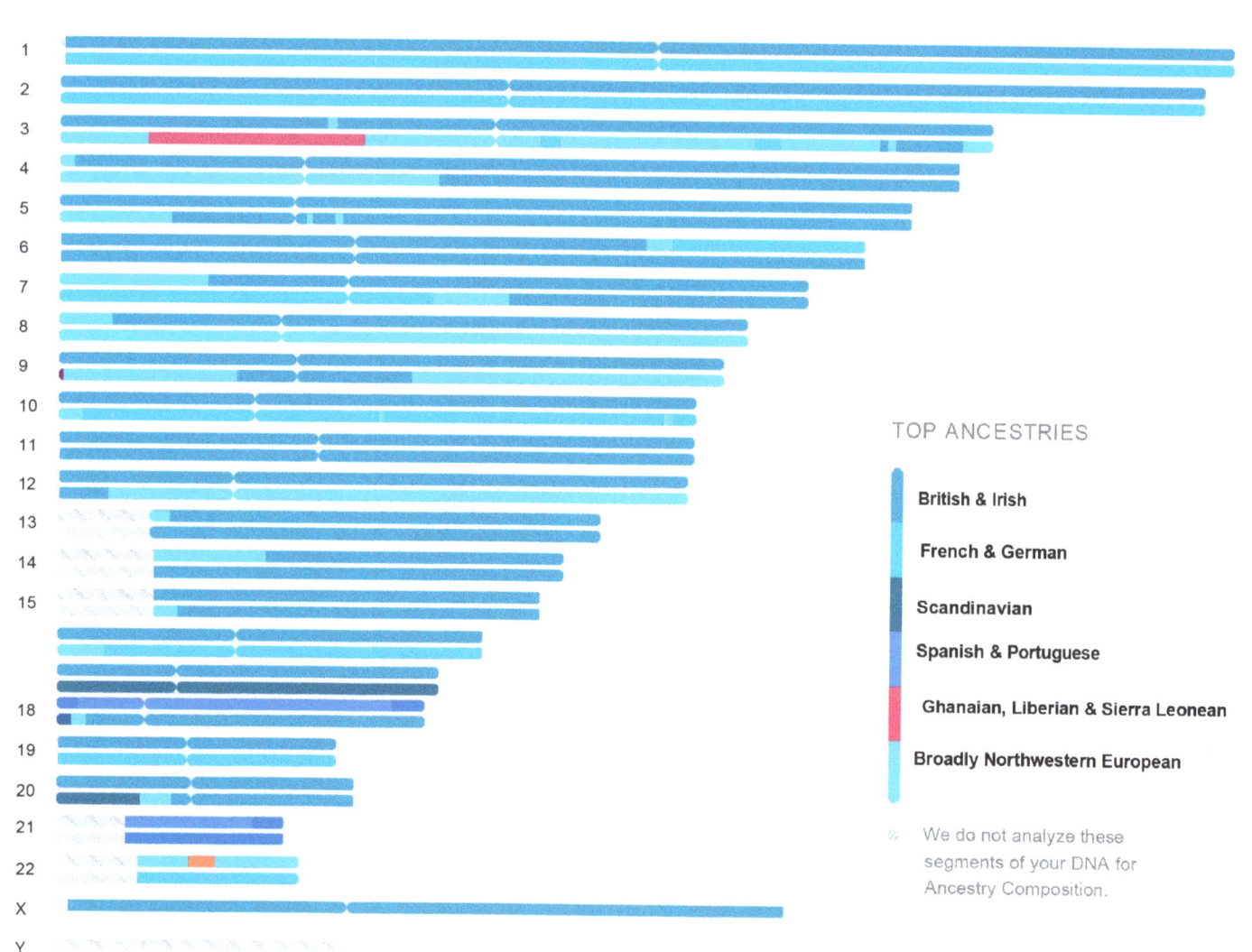

TOP ANCESTRIES

British & Irish

French & German

Scandinavian

Spanish & Portuguese

Ghanaian, Liberian & Sierra Leonean

Broadly Northwestern European

We do not analyze these segments of your DNA for Ancestry Composition.

**FRENCH & GERMAN**

The Hallstatt, Austria in autumn.

Great grandmother

randmother

# MATERNAL HAPLOGROUP

Your maternal haplogroup refers to a unique set of genetic variations in your mitochondrial DNA that have been passed down to you for thousands of years through your maternal line — from your great-grandmother to your grandmother to your mother, and so on.

# Everett, your maternal haplogroup is U5a1.

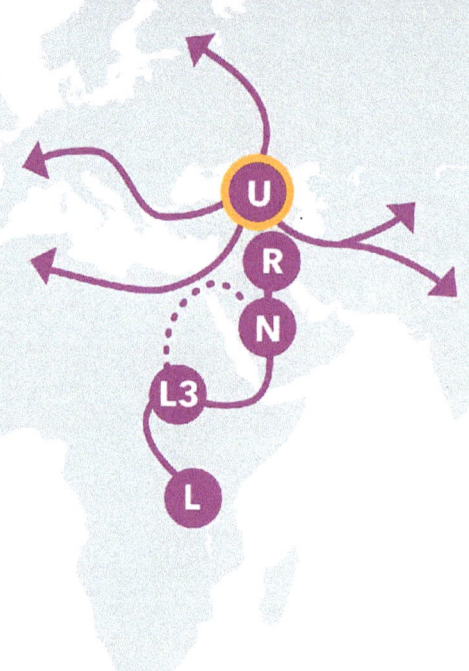

## WHAT IS A MATERNAL HAPLOGROUP?

As our ancestors ventured out of eastern Africa, they branched off in diverse groups that crossed and recrossed the globe over tens of thousands of years. Your maternal haplogroup can reveal the path followed by the women of your maternal line.

### 180,000 Years Ago Haplogroup L

If every person living today could trace his or her maternal line back over thousands of generations, all of our lines would meet at a single woman who lived in eastern Africa between 150,000 and 200,000 years ago. Though she was one of perhaps thousands of women alive at the time, only the diverse branches of her haplogroup have survived to today. The story of your maternal line begins with her.

### 65,000 Years Ago Haplogroup L3

Your branch of L is haplogroup L3, which arose from a woman who likely lived in eastern Africa between 60,000 and 70,000 years ago. While many of her descendants remained in Africa, one small group ventured east across the Red Sea, likely across the narrow Bab-el-Mandeb into the tip of the Arabian Peninsula.

### 59,000 Years Ago Haplogroup N

Your story continues with haplogroup N, one of two branches that arose from L3 in southwestern Asia. Researchers have long debated whether they arrived there via the Sinai Peninsula, or made the hop across the Red Sea at the Bab-el- Mandeb. Though their exact routes are disputed, there is no doubt that the women of haplogroup N migrated across all of Eurasia, giving rise to new branches from Portugal to Polynesia.

### 57,000 Years Ago Haplogroup R

One of those branches is haplogroup R, which traces back to a woman who lived soon after the migration out of Africa. She likely lived in southwest Asia, perhaps in the Arabian peninsula, and her descendants lived and migrated alongside members of haplogroup N. Along the way, R gave rise to a number of branches that are major haplogroups in their own right.

### 47,000 Years Ago Haplogroup U

Haplogroup U was one of the earliest offshoots of R, and traces back to a woman who lived nearly 50,000 years ago. Over time, her descendants have migrated into Europe, parts of Asia, and even back into Africa, giving rise to numerous branches spanning the three continents.

# THE CHEDDAR MAN ALSO BELONGED TO U5A

First discovered in 1903 in Cheddar Gorge, Somerset, England, the Cheddar Man is Britain's oldest complete human  skeleton. Researchers have dated his bones back to nearly 9,000 years ago, when the Ice Age had ended but farming technology had not yet made its way across the continent, and people in England still survived by hunting and gathering. Unfortunately for the Cheddar Man, a bone lesion above his right eye shows he likely had a bone infection, and other skeletal evidence suggests his days of hunting may have come to a violent end.

More recently, Bryan Sykes of Oxford University extracted mitochondrial DNA from one of the Cheddar Man's teeth, and found that his maternal haplogroup was U5.

Pictured below: The Cheddar Man is named for Cheddar Gorge, England.

## 17,000 Years Ago Haplogroup U5a1

Haplogroup U5a1 is a branch of U5, one of the oldest haplogroups in Europe. The common ancestor of U5a1 was a woman who likely lived in Europe during the Ice Age, about 17,000 years ago. At the time people were confined to small refuges in the southern part of the continent. When the glaciers began receding about 15,000 years ago people began migrating northward, carrying U5a1 and other haplogroups with them. Today U5a1 is most commonly found in places such as Norway and northern Germany.

Other members of the U5a1 haplogroup moved south into the Middle East, perhaps in search of a warmer, more hospitable climate than the dry, glaciated tundra of Ice Age Europe. Today their maternal descendants can be found at low levels (less than 2%) in Turkey, Iran, and Syria.

## 17,000 Years Ago Haplogroup U5a1

Your maternal haplogroup, U5a1, traces back to a woman who lived approximately 17,000 years ago. That's nearly 680 generations ago! What happened between then and now? As researchers and citizen scientists discover more about your haplogroup, new details may be added to the story of your maternal line.

## Today Haplogroup U5a1

U5a1 is frequent among 23andMe customers. Today, you share your haplogroup with all the maternal-line descendants of the common ancestor of U5a1, including other 23andMe customers.

**1 in 140**

23andMe customers share your haplogroup assignment

# THE GENETICS OF MATERNAL HAPLOGROUPS

Mitochondrial DNA

Maternal haplogroups are determined by sets of genetic variants in a tiny, unusual loop of DNA called mitochondrial DNA (mtDNA). As the name suggests, mtDNA is found in the mitochondria, small but mighty structures inside our cells that turn fuel from the food we eat into energy.

Mitochondria evolved over billions of years from an independent bacterial cell that was engulfed by another cell. Instead of becoming lunch, the bacterium helped its new host use oxygen to produce energy. Over time it completely lost its independence and became an integrated part of the larger cell.

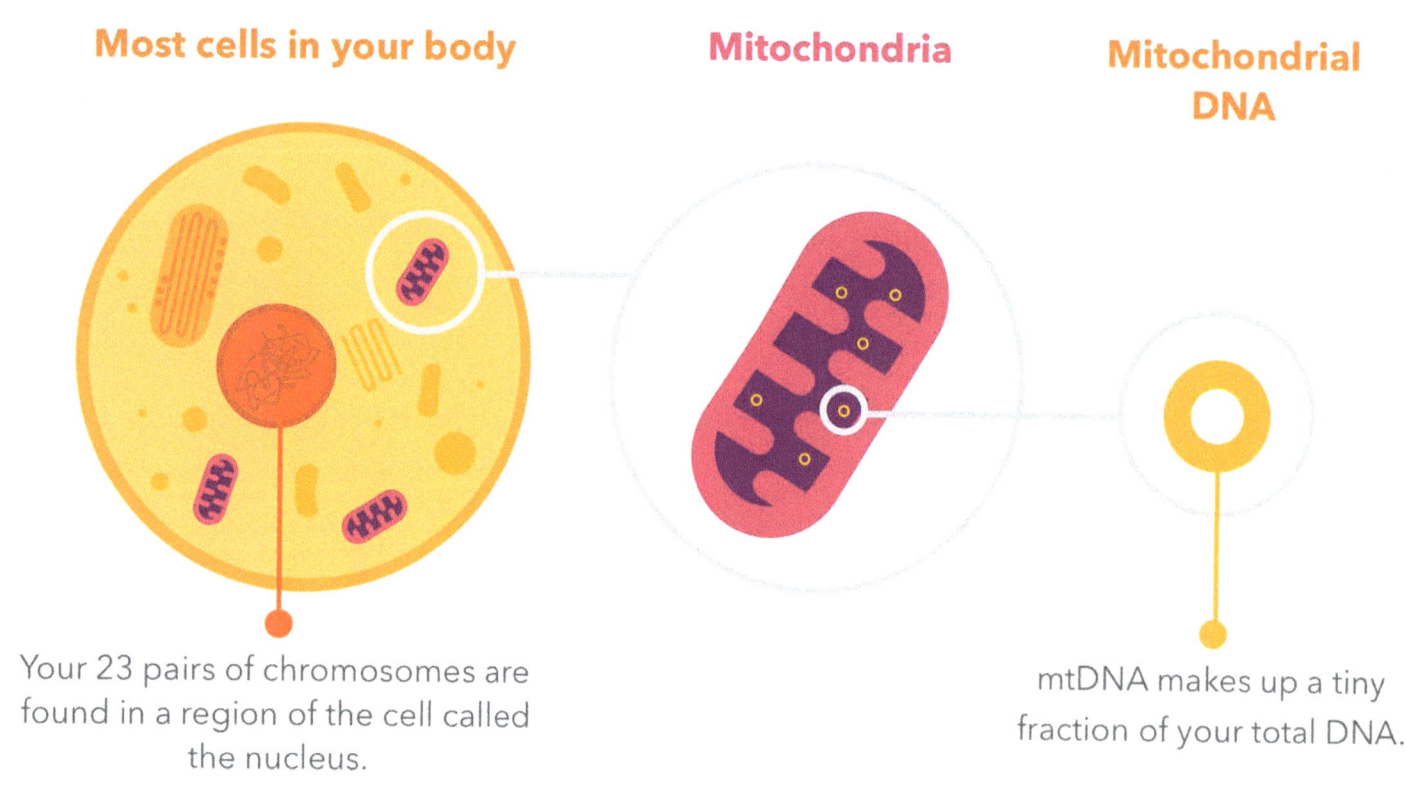

**Most cells in your body**

**Mitochondria**

**Mitochondrial DNA**

Your 23 pairs of chromosomes are found in a region of the cell called the nucleus.

mtDNA makes up a tiny fraction of your total DNA.

## Maternal Inheritance

Mitochondrial DNA is a powerful tool for tracing the history of maternal lines because of the way it is inherited: everyone has mtDNA, but only mothers pass it down to their children. So, you inherited a copy of your mother's mtDNA, who inherited it from her mother, who inherited it from hers, and so on through the generations along an unbroken line of women.

The copies passed down are not always perfectly identical, however. Small typos in the mtDNA sequence occasionally occur, creating new genetic variants. Over many generations, these variants stack up in unique patterns that are carried by different maternal lines around the world.

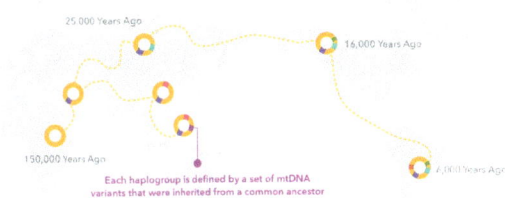

## Tracing Female Migrations

Geneticists study the relationships between haplogroups and compare them with the distribution of each group around the world. Because closely related haplogroups tend to share geographic roots, researchers can play a sophisticated version of connect-the-dots to estimate the origins and migration patterns of particular haplogroups.

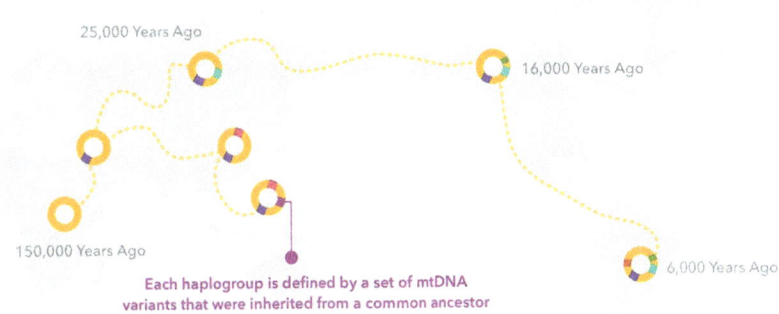

Combining this genetic evidence with data from other fields of study helps researchers place the story of each maternal line within the broader context of human history.

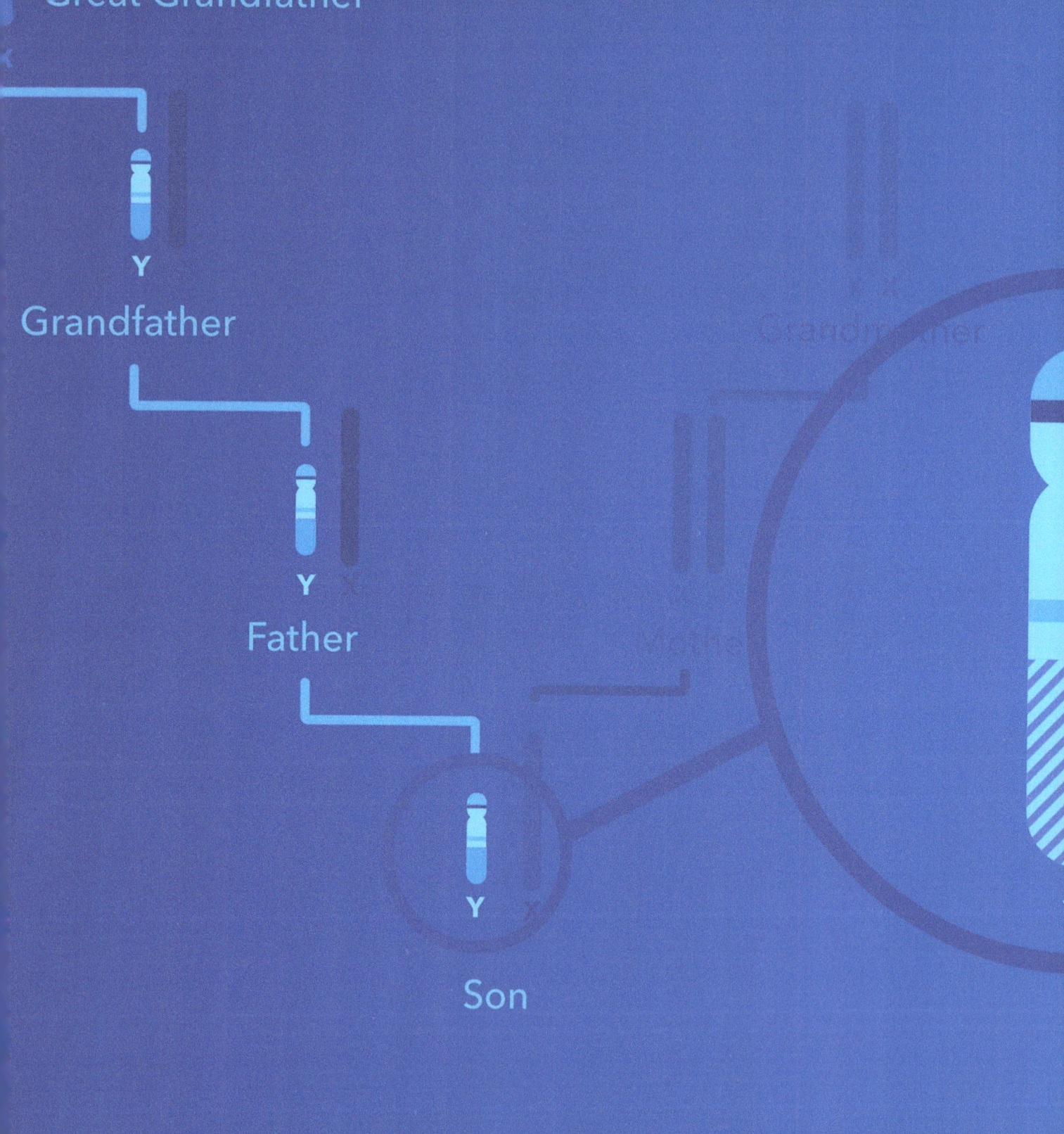

# PATERNAL HAPLOGROUP

Your paternal haplogroup assignment is based on genetic variants in your Y chromosome DNA (or on the Y chromosome of a male-line relative like your dad). These variants — a unique genetic signature inherited from a common paternal-line ancestor — are shared among the members of your haplogroup.

# Everett, your paternal Haplogroup is **E-V13.**

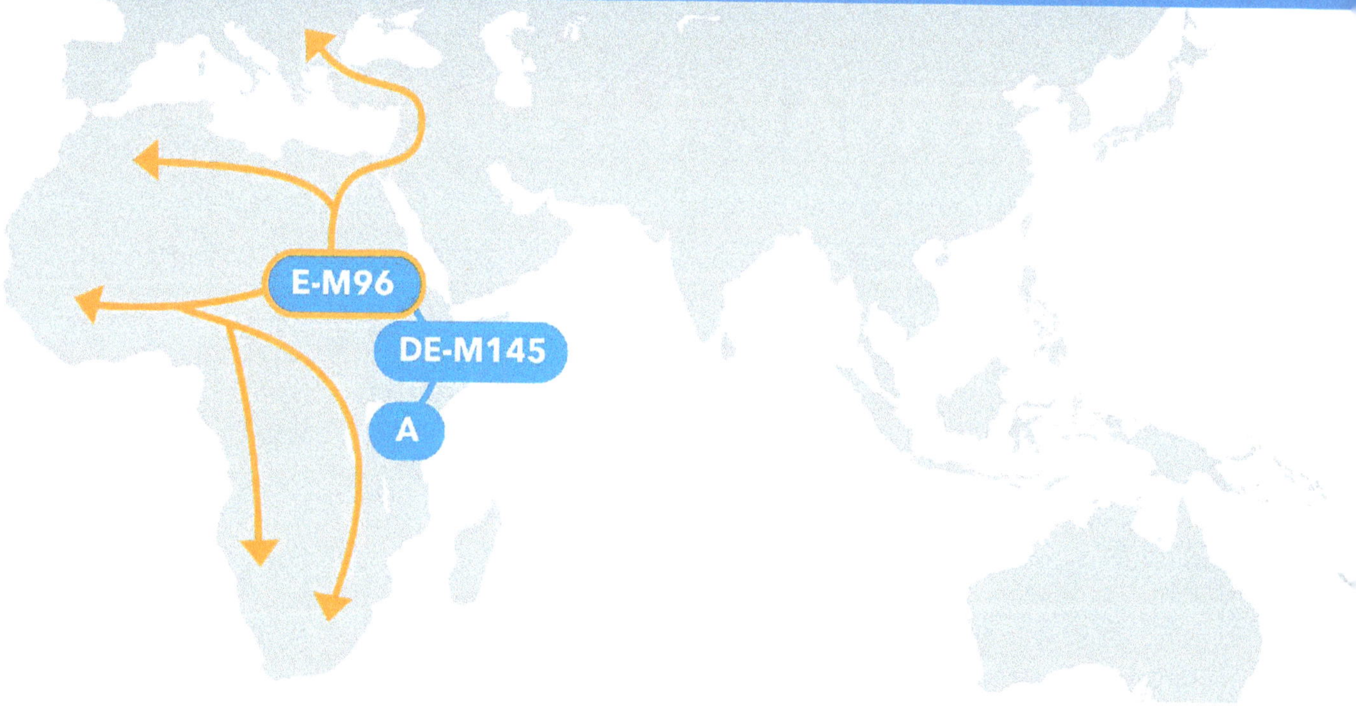

E-M96

DE-M145

A

## WHAT IS A MATERNAL HAPLOGROUP?

As our ancestors ventured out of eastern Africa, they branched off in diverse groups that crossed and recrossed the globe over tens of thousands of years. Your maternal haplogroup can reveal the path followed by the women of your maternal line.

## 275,000 Years Ago Haplogroup A

The stories of all of our paternal lines can be traced back over 275,000 years to just one man: the common ancestor of haplogroup A. Current evidence suggests he was one of thousands of men who lived in eastern Africa at the time. However, while his male-line descendants passed down their Y chromosomes generation after generation, the lineages from the other men died out. Over time his lineage alone gave rise to all other haplogroups that exist today.

## 76,000 Years Ago Haplogroup DE-M145

The first steps of your paternal-line ancestors lead from eastern Africa north towards the Red Sea and haplogroup DE- M145. The DE lineage branched away from its brothers around 65,000 years ago, among the first of our ancestors to cross out of Africa into the Arabian Peninsula. Most descendants of the DE lineage belong to one of its two branches, D and E. Men carrying D moved east into Asia and those with E moved west through Africa and into Europe.

## 73,000 Years Ago Haplogroup E-M96

Your path branched off again over 60,000 years ago with the rise of haplogroup E-M96, also simply called haplogroup E. The common ancestor of E-M96 may have lived in northeastern Africa or in the Arabian Peninsula. Since then, his descendants have carried it throughout the African continent and into neighboring regions of Europe and the Middle East.

## 23,000 Years Ago Haplogroup E-M78

Your paternal line stems from the common ancestor of haplogroup E-M78, a branch of E that dates back approximately 24,000 years. The earliest carriers of the E-M78 lineage likely lived in a population that moved from eastern Africa into northeastern Africa about 14,000 years ago, during the final days of the Ice Age. From northeastern Africa, their descendants expanded to the west between the Sahara and the Mediterranean coastline, and to the east out of Africa into the Middle East, where E-M78 men remain common.

Today, men bearing this haplogroup are also common in southern Europe, including in the Balkans, Iberia, and Italy. In Greece, Bulgaria, and Albania, between 15% and 30% of men bear haplogroup E-M78. Their ancestors were likely relatively late arrivals to the region. While some branches of haplogroup E were carried into Europe nearly 8,000 years ago, recent research suggests that the major spread of E-M78 occurred in the last 5,000 years or so during the Bronze Age. Bronze Age cultures learned to smelt tin and copper to create beautiful and complex bronze items like hardier tools and weapons. They journeyed along

river waterways in the Balkans and spread into east-central Europe. Today, men from Ukraine, Hungary, Romania, and Slovakia all carry E-M78 at levels of nearly 10%.

While the majority of E-M78 European males trace their recent ancestry to Turkey and the Middle East, some men carrying E-M78 from Spain, Italy and Greece trace their ancestry directly from North African populations, probably within the last 4,000 years. The ancestors of these men must have sailed across the Mediterranean Sea and settled in communities along the European coast.

## 11,000 Years Ago Haplogroup E-V13

Your paternal haplogroup, E-V13, traces back to a man who lived approximately 11,000 years ago. That's nearly 440 generations ago! What happened between then and now? As researchers and citizen scientists discover more about your haplogroup, new details may be added to the story of your paternal line.

## Today Haplogroup E-V13

E-V13 is relatively common among 23andMe customers. Today, you share your haplogroup with all the paternal-line descendants of the common ancestor of E-V13, including other 23andMe customers.

### 1 in 43

23andMe customers share your
haplogroup assignment

## YOUR HAPLOGROUP SPREAD THROUGH THE BALKANS DURING THE BRONZE AGE.

Your haplogroup migrated in large numbers from the Balkans into Europe about 4,500 years ago, triggered by the beginning of the Balkan Bronze Age. During this migration, members of your haplogroup mainly followed rivers connecting the southern Balkans to northern-central Europe. Technological leaps often cause lineages to grow dramatically in numbers and in geographic range. The development of Bronze technology may have given men in your lineage a competitive advantage over other men, causing your lineage to proliferate and become widespread.

# THE GENETICS OF PATERNAL HAPLOGROUPS

## The Y Chromosome

Most of the DNA in your body is packaged into 23 pairs of chromosomes. The first 22 pairs are matching, meaning that they contain roughly the same DNA inherited from both parents. The 23rd pair is different because in men, the pair does not match. The chromosomes in this pair are known as "sex" chromosomes and they have different names: X and Y. Typically, women have two X chromosomes and men have one X and one Y.

Your genetic sex is determined by which sex chromosome you inherited from your father. If you are genetically male, you received a copy of your father's Y chromosome along with a gene known as SRY (short for sex-determining region Y) that is important for male sexual development. If you are genetically female, you received a copy of the X chromosome from both of your parents.

**The Y chromosome is used to determine paternal haplogroups**

Females: X X

Males: X Y

SRY gene
Determines male sex

Y

## Paternal Inheritance

Each generation, fathers pass down copies of their Y chromosomes to their sons essentially unchanged. Between generations, the matching chromosomes in the other 22 pairs make contact and exchange segments of DNA. This process shuffles the genetic information that is passed down from parent to child, making it difficult to trace genealogy over many generations. Except for two tiny sections at the chromosome's tips, however, the Y chromosome skips this step. Instead, a nearly identical copy is handed down each time.

But, every so often, small changes to the DNA sequence do occur. These changes, called mutations, create new genetic variants on the Y chromosome. Because the Y chromosome does not recombine between generations, these variants collect in patterns that uniquely mark individual paternal lineages.

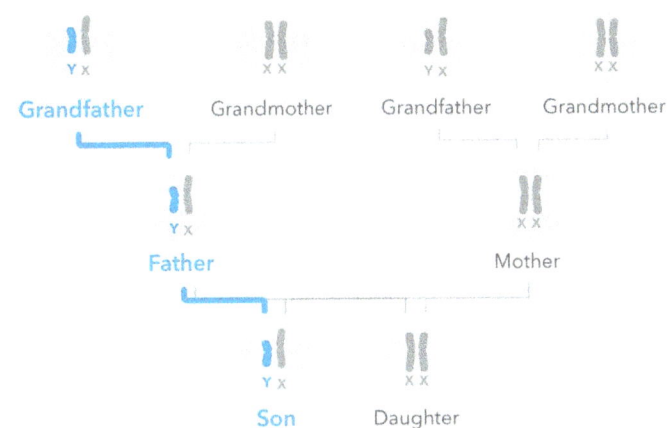

**Fathers pass their Y chromosome down to their sons**

Grandfather  Grandmother  Grandfather  Grandmother

Father  Mother

Son  Daughter

## Tracing Female Migrations

Because closely related haplogroups tend to share geographic roots, researchers can use the modern distributions of haplogroups around the world to trace major migrations, from the voyage to Australia over 40,000 years ago to the peopling of North and South America in the last 19,000 years.

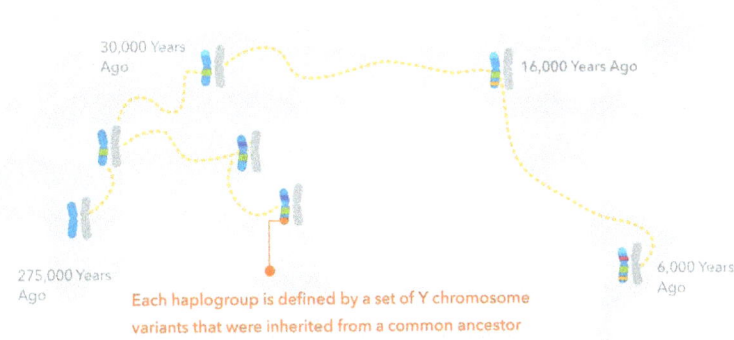

30,000 Years Ago

16,000 Years Ago

275,000 Years Ago

6,000 Years Ago

Each haplogroup is defined by a set of Y chromosome variants that were inherited from a common ancestor

# NEANDERTHAL ANCESTRY

Neanderthals (Homo neanderthalensis) were a group of ancient humans who interbred with modern humans (Homo sapiens) in Europe and Asia before becoming extinct around 40,000 years ago. Neanderthals looked a little different from us, and are thought to have exhibited complex social behaviors. This section reveals how much of your ancestry can be traced back to our ancient evolutionary cousins, the Neanderthals.

# NEANDERTHAL ANCESTRY

## Everett, you have 240 Neanderthal variants.

You have fewer Neanderthal variants than 87% of 23andMe customers. However, your Neanderthal ancestry accounts for less than 4% of your overall DNA.

# SOME OF YOUR TRAITS MAY BE INFLUENCED BY HAVING NEANDERTHAL VARIANTS.

Scientists at 23andMe identified associations between Neanderthal variants and certain physical traits. If you have certain Neanderthal variants, it means that some of your physical traits may trace back to your Neanderthal ancestors.

Variant(s) found

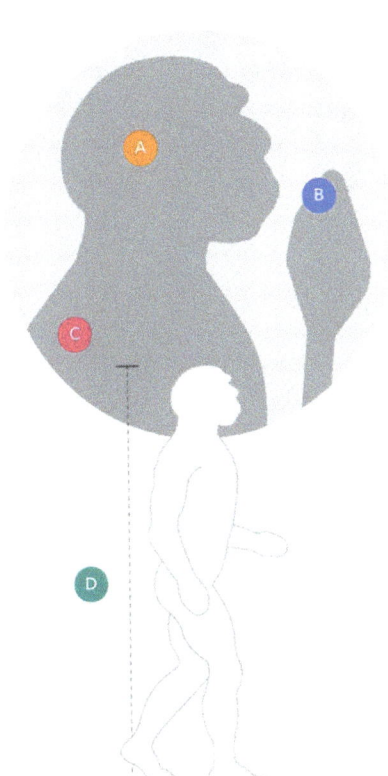

**A Straight hair**     0

You have 0 Neanderthal variants associated with having straighter hair.

**B Less likely to sneeze after eating dark chocolate**     1

You have 1 Neanderthal variant associated with sneezing after eating dark chocolate.

**C Less back hair**     1

You have 1 Neanderthal variant associated with having less back hair.

**D Height**     1

You have 1 Neanderthal variant associated with your height.

# A BRIEF HISTORY OF NEANDERTHALS

## Introduction

Over the past 150 years, scientists have found bones belonging to an extinct population of ancient humans. These ancient humans are known as Neanderthals and were named after the site where their bones were first identified (Neander Valley, Germany). Neanderthals and modern humans share a common ancestor as well as many morphological and social traits, but differed in key respects. Over the past decade, genome sequencing has shed more light on Neanderthals and our complicated relationship with them.

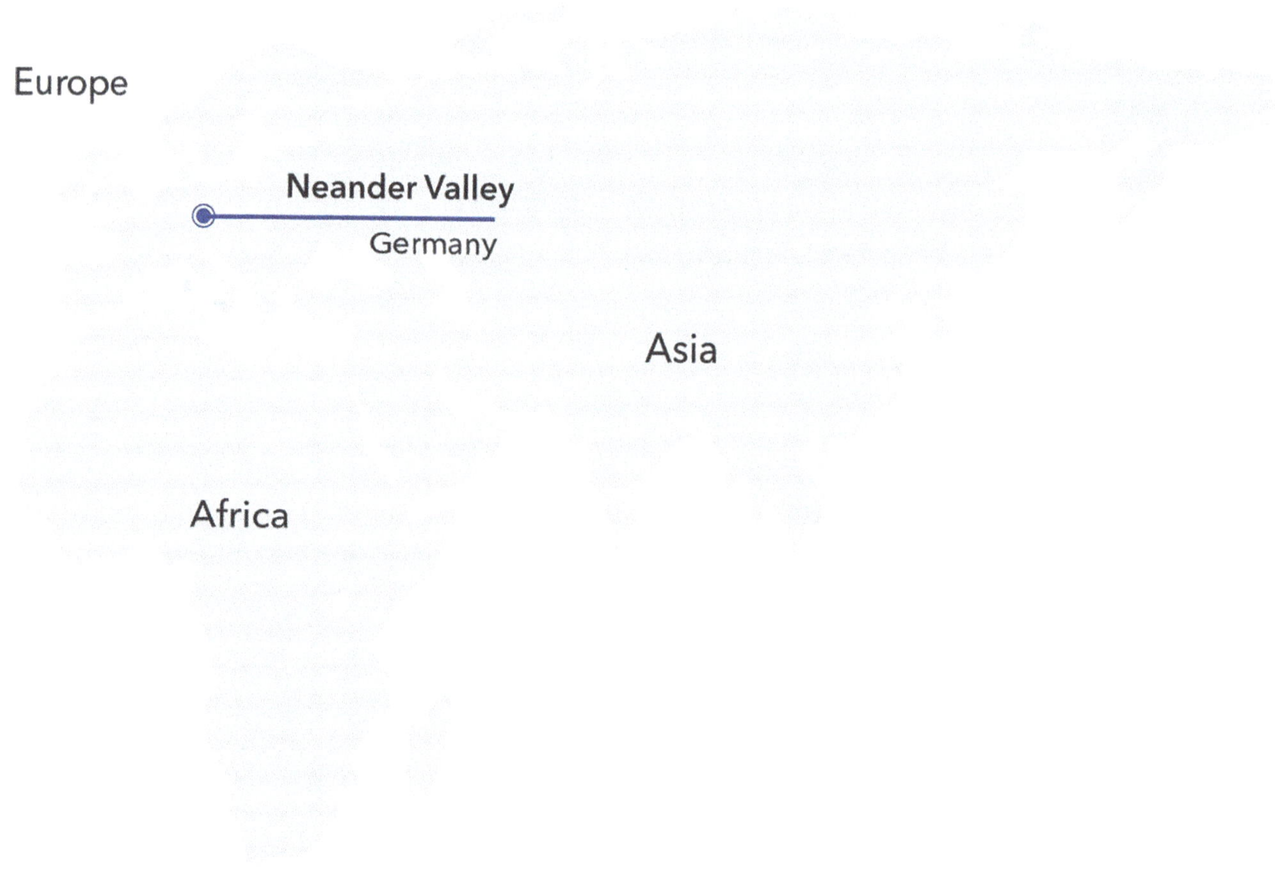

Europe

**Neander Valley**

Germany

Asia

Africa

## 600,000 Years Ago

### Neanderthals and Modern Humans Share a Common Ancestor

The common ancestor of modern humans and Neanderthals is thought to be an extinct hominin named Homo heidelbergensis. The species inhabited much of Africa, Europe and probably Asia from at least 700,000 years ago until about 200,000 years ago.

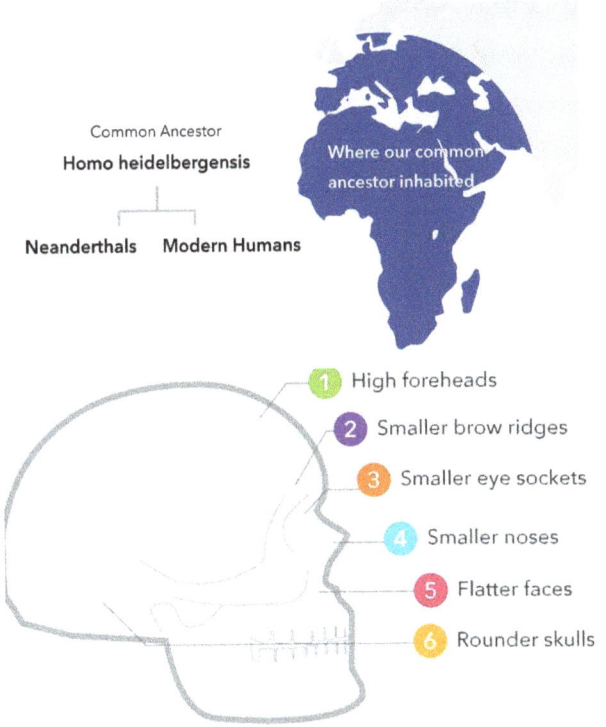

## 300,000 Years Ago - Africa

### Modern Humans Evolve Within Africa

*Homo heidelbergensis* continued to evolve in Africa, eventually becoming anatomically-modern humans. The oldest remains that can be ascribed to anatomically-modern humans come from a site named Jebel Irhoud in Morocco that dates to 300,000 years ago.

## 200,000 Years Ago - Eurasia

### Neanderthals Evolve Outside of Africa

By about 200,000 years ago, the European branch of the *Homo heidelbergensis* population had evolved into what we refer to as Neanderthals. Contrary to the popular "caveman" stereotype, Neanderthals were a lot like modern humans and exhibited complex social behaviors. The most distinctive characteristics of Neanderthal remains are their wide, robust bodies, relatively short limbs, and projecting mid-faces.

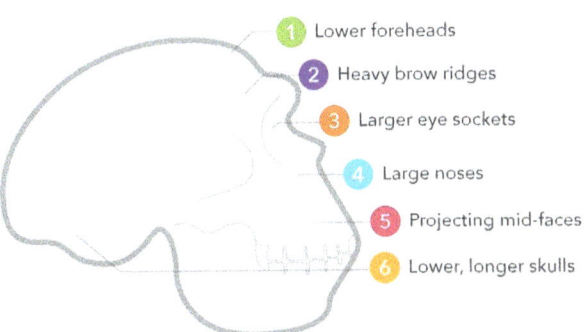

# WHAT DID THE NEANDERTHALS EAT?

Contrary to popular notions of the "caveman diet," Neanderthals were not all die-hard carnivores. Rather, our ancient relatives adapted their diets to match the resources that were readily available and most nutritious.

Two Neanderthal individuals found in a cave in El Sidrón, Spain had traces of pine nuts, moss, tree barks, and mushrooms in their dental plaques, suggesting a mostly vegetarian diet. The dental plaques of another Neanderthal found in Spy, Belgium, pointed to a diet of meat and mushrooms – a conclusion supported by the bones of mammoths, reindeer, and horses also found in the Spy cave. Bones found at other Neanderthal sites suggest Neanderthals focused on hunting large mammals rather than small game like rabbits. Other research reports that Neanderthals living on the Gibraltar coast may have eaten various mollusks, seals, and even dolphins. In summary, Neanderthals adapted their diets to meet the resources provided by their environments.

## Neanderthals found in Spy, Belgium ate:

SPY, BELGIUM

## Neanderthals found in El Sidrón, Spain ate:

Mushrooms

Seeds & Nuts

EL SIDRÓN, SPAIN

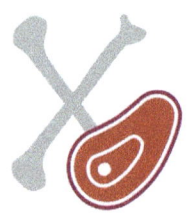

Large mammals

Mushrooms

Moss & Bark

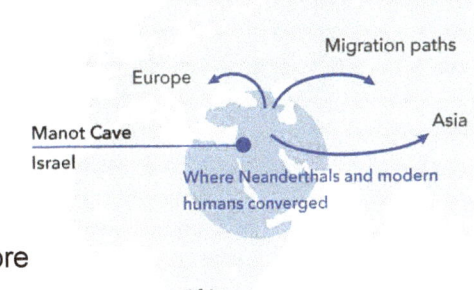

## 60,000 Years Ago

### Neanderthals and Modern Humans Converge

Around 60,000 years ago, modern humans started to explore beyond Africa, encountering and interbreeding with their Neanderthal neighbors. Skeletal remains found in the Manot Cave in Israel and elsewhere suggest that these two groups likely interbred in the Middle East or Europe. Their descendants radiated out across Europe, Asia, Australia, and eventually the Americas.

## Today

### African and Non-African Populations Differ in Their Neanderthal Ancestry

Neanderthal ancestry in present-day populations is largely derived from these ancient migrations and interbreeding events. Non-African populations have Neanderthal ancestry amounting to about 1-2% of their genomes. With few exceptions, Sub-Saharan African populations have virtually no Neanderthal ancestry. Average numbers from the 23andMe database are shown to illustrate this difference.

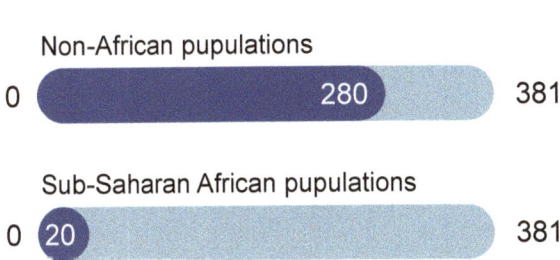

Average number of Neanderthal variants

Non-African pupulations

0   280   381

Sub-Saharan African pupulations

0   20   381

YOU

# YOUR DNA RELATIVES

So far, your reports have looked to the past, tracing your DNA across continents and millennia. The origins of your DNA link you to a growing number of genetic relatives, many of whom are alive today and hold clues about your common ancestors.

# We've found **1217** of your DNA Relatives who have used 23andMe.

Your DNA Relatives are people with whom you share a recent ancestor. This common ancestor may have lived up to nine generations ago.

For context, you share about 12% of your DNA with a first cousin, 3% with a second cousin, and 1% with a third cousin. This percentage continues to decrease the further back in time your common ancestor lived.

6th great grandparents +

5th great grandparents +

4th great grandparents

3rd great grandparents

2nd great grandparents

Great grandparents

Grandparents

Parents

You | Siblings | 1st cousins | 2nd cousins | 3rd cousins | 4th cousins | 5th cousins | 6th cousins | 7th + cousins

**34**
Close Family to Second Cousins

**1183**
Third-Fourth Cousins

**Many**
Fifth-Distant Cousins

## TRAITS OF YOUR RELATIVES

Compared to the average 23andMe customer, your DNA Relatives are...

 **102%** more likely to feel jittery after drinking caffeine

 **62%** more likely to have lived near a farm when they were young

 **52%** less likely to be a vegetarian

 **45%** more likely to drink caffeinated soda

 **42%** more likely to have sweaty palms

 **36%** more likely to own a dog

 **35%** more likely to be able to do the side splits

 **32%** less likely to drink instant coffee

 **30%** less likely to drink espresso drinks

 **30%** less likely to like the taste of dark licorice

 **30%** more likely to sneeze when exposed to bright light

# HOW COMMON IS EACH ANCESTRY AMONG YOUR DNA RELATIVES?

Compare your unique mix of ancestries to those of your DNA Relatives. You may be able to infer new insights into the origins of your common ancestors. The table below reflects your relatives with at least 1% of each ancestry.

| RANK | ANCESTRY | NUMBER OF DNA RELATIVES WITH 1% OF ANCESTRY |
|------|----------|---------------------------------------------|
| 1 | British & Irish | 1.2K |
| 2 | French & German | 1.2K |
| 3 | Scandinavian | 915 |
| 4 | Spanish & Portuguese | 285 |
| 5 | Eastern European | 180 |
| 6 | Italian | 115 |
| 7 | West African | 100 |
| 8 | Native American | 75 |
| 9 | Greek & Balkan | 70 |
| 10 | Finnish | 45 |

# MAPPING YOUR RELATIVES

Your DNA Relatives' blend of ancestries and geographic locations may reveal how your ancestors migrated around the country (and world) within the last 200 years. While the largest number of your relatives live in Kentucky, you also have relatives who live in California, Ohio, and Indiana.

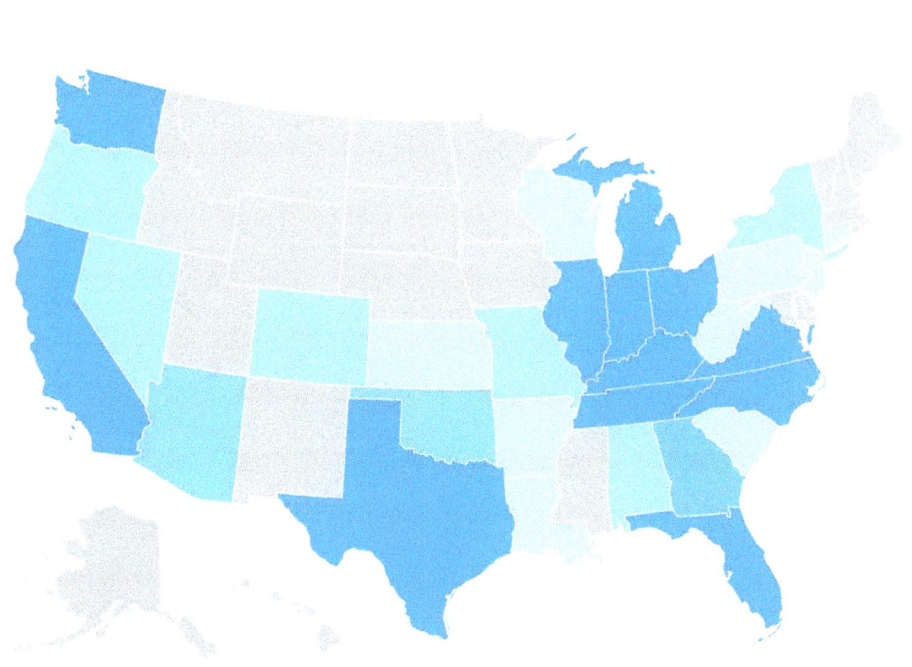

| TOP STATES | | NUMBER OF DNA RELATIVES |
| --- | --- | --- |
| 1. | Kentucky | 85 |
| 2. | California | 80 |
| 3. | Ohio | 65 |
| 4. | Indiana | 60 |
| 5. | Florida | 45 |
| 6. | Texas | 40 |
| 7. | Tennessee | 35 |
| 8. | Michigan | 30 |
| 9. | Virginia | 30 |
| 10. | Illinois | 25 |

*Map is based on 23andMe customers and reflects our database at the time your book was printed.*

African Hunter-Gatherer: African hunter-gatherer populations — including the Pygmy and San peoples of central and southern Africa — represent some of the oldest and most genetically distinct branches in the human family tree. The historically semi-nomadic San peoples of the Kalahari and the closely-related Khoe herders in Namibia, Botswana, and South Africa, speak languages characterized by click consonants rarely found in other language families. Pygmy peoples of the central African rainforests, on the other hand, have lost their distinct linguistic heritage, but have preserved many unique cultural traditions.

Ashkenazi Jewish: Ashkenazi Jewish people settled in Central and Eastern Europe in the late Middle Ages, but their modern descendants remain genetically more similar to other Jewish populations than to their European neighbors, reflecting shared western Asian origins. In the twentieth century, many Ashkenazi Jewish people immigrated to Israel or to the Americas in search of greater cultural and religious acceptance. Today, over five million ethnic Ashkenazi Jewish people live in the U.S.

Balkan: The Balkan Peninsula is nestled in the southeastern corner of Europe and serves as the geographic and genetic crossroads between Europe and western Asia. Despite broad cultural and religious diversity, the people of the Balkans are genetically similar to one another, descending from early Mediterranean and Slavic peoples. Island Greeks lack this ancestral Slavic influence and are similar to southern Italians.

British & Irish: The British Isles have been continuously occupied by humans for the last 11,000 years, but more recently, the people of the Isles have left their genetic fingerprints around the world, following centuries of nautical exploration, colonization, and immigration. In the early 20th century, the Republic of Ireland won its independence from the United Kingdom, but the people of these nations share a common genetic heritage rooted largely in Celtic, Anglo-Saxon, and Viking migrations from northwestern Europe.

Broadly Chinese & Southeast Asian: From the expansive plains of central Asia to the islands of eastern Indonesia, the people of China and Southeast Asia share genetic similarities dating back to the arrival of humans in the region over 40,000 years ago. Broadly Chinese & Southeast Asian DNA – likely driven in part by the spread of agriculture within the last few thousand years – matches several specific populations and is difficult to assign to just one.

Broadly Congolese & Southern East African: Starting around 3,000 years ago, Bantu speakers carried metallurgy and agriculture from the highlands of Nigeria and Cameroon in two major streams – one southward and one eastward – resulting in ancestry that transcends geopolitical borders. "Bantu" is a term widely used to describe the largest of Africa's ethnolinguistic families. Likely as a result of these rapid and widespread expansions across Central and Eastern Africa, it is difficult to assign a specific location within Sub-Saharan Africa to some chromosomal segments with a high degree of confidence.

Broadly East Asian & Native American: The peoples of East Asia and the Americas have a shared genetic history. Their common ancestors left western Asia over 50,000 years ago, migrating east across the continent. The ancestors of Native Americans began to cross into the Americas 12,000 to 15,000 years ago. Broadly East Asian & Native American DNA is a relic of this ancient population split, and reflects shared roots in central and northern Asia.

Broadly European: Much of Europe was buried under miles of ice ten thousand years ago. As the glaciers receded over millennia, Neolithic farmers from western Asia joined Paleolithic hunter-gatherers to settle Europe. Some European DNA is difficult to assign confidently to one population and receives a 'Broadly' designation.

Broadly Japanese & Korean: The people of Japan and the Korean Peninsula share a genetic heritage that dates back to the first arrival of Stone Age hunter-gatherers from Siberia, and to later migrations of Iron Age rice farmers from the south. Broadly Japanese & Korean DNA is a remnant of this ancient population history and is difficult to assign to Korean or Japanese ancestry alone. More recently, the region has been shaped by a rich history of artistic, literary, architectural, and scientific exchange.

Broadly Melanesian: Melanesia was first peopled by seafaring voyagers over 45,000 years ago, when the ancestors of indigenous Australian and Papuan peoples reached Near Oceania from Indonesia. These early Melanesians interbred with a now-extinct hominin species – the Denisovans – and their descendants harbor traces of this ancient encounter in their DNA.

Broadly Northern Asian & Native American: Dispersed across three continents, the peoples of Northern Asia and the Americas have deeply- rooted genetic similarities, reflecting a history of widespread and rapid migrations across the vast central Asian plains, Siberia, and eventually into the Americas across the Bering land bridge. Subtle linguistic affinities reveal ancient links between some Native American languages and languages still spoken in Siberia. Broadly Northern Asian & Native American DNA is a relic of this ancient population split, and is difficult to assign to a specific region.

Broadly Northern East African: Northeast Africa, which here spans from Sudan in the northwest to Ethiopia and Somalia in the southeast, is home to both Afro-Asiatic and Nilo-Saharan ethnolinguistic groups. The entire region has a rich history of genetic and cultural exchange between indigenous East Africans and immigrants from the Arabian Peninsula. As a result of both ancient and recent migrations within the region, broadly Northeast African DNA may be difficult to assign to a specific location.

Broadly Northwestern European: Northwestern European ancestry is represented by people from as far west as Ireland, as far north as Norway, as far east as Finland, and as far south as France. These countries rim the North and Baltic Seas, and have been connected throughout much of history by those waters. Broadly Northwestern European DNA matches several specific populations and is difficult to assign to just one. This shared heritage may be a result of extensive migration, possibly including the Germanic invasions of the early Middle Ages.

Broadly South Asian: South Asia is represented here by the diverse populations of India, Sri Lanka, Pakistan, Afghanistan, Nepal, Bhutan, and Bangladesh. Scientists believe that when modern humans first left Africa, they traveled along the coast of southern Asia, populating parts of the region over 50,000 years ago. During the last few thousand years, the genetic and cultural landscape of South Asia has shifted following migrations from the North and West.

Broadly Southern European: Southern Europe, which includes the Iberian, Italian, and Balkan peninsulas as well as the island of Malta, is a region defined in great part by the Mediterranean Sea. The Mediterranean has provided transportation routes, keeping these regions connected culturally and genetically. Broadly Southern European DNA matches several specific populations and is difficult to assign to just one.

Broadly Sub-Saharan African: The genetic diversity of Sub-Saharan Africa reflects both the deep history of humans in the region and the recent migrations that have carried people from western Africa to both southern and eastern Africa. As a result of this ancient and complex population history, it is difficult to assign some DNA to a specific population within Sub-Saharan Africa.

Broadly West African: For over a millennium before European colonization and the Atlantic slave trade, West Africans were united under a series of powerful empires, resulting in broad similarities in music, clothing, art, and cuisine. A gradient of genetic similarity extending from Senegal to Nigeria reflects a richly complex population history in a region home to over 350 million people who form hundreds of distinct ethnic groups.

Broadly West African DNA may match several populations, making it difficult to assign to just one.

Broadly Western Asian & North African: The peoples of western Asia and North Africa have not only genetic but also deep linguistic connections with one another. Broadly Western Asian & North African DNA reflects shared roots possibly dating back to some of the earliest migrations out of Africa. The spread of Islam in the past 1,400 years has also dramatically shaped the region's genetic landscape, making it difficult to assign some DNA to just one population.

Chinese: China is home to one of the world's earliest and most enduring civilizations, with over 50 officially-recognized ethnic groups. The Han ethnic group makes up 92% of the country's population, and includes nearly one-fifth of all humans in the world. Over 50 million ethnic Chinese live outside of China, with over 20 million in Thailand, Malaysia, and the United States alone.

Chinese Dai: The Dai people of southern China belong to the larger Tai ethnolinguistic group that currently lives in parts of China, Burma, Laos, Vietnam, and Thailand. In China, the Dai are one of over 50 officially recognized ethnic minority groups, and are united by unique cultural traditions anchored in Dai Folk Religion or Buddhism. Most Chinese Dai live in southern and western Yunnan Province, and are genetically more similar to their Vietnamese neighbors than they are to the Han Chinese.

Coastal West African: A continuum of genetic diversity stretches from Senegal to Nigeria, but the people of the coastal countries above the Gulf of Guinea — Sierra Leone, Liberia, Côte d'Ivoire, and Ghana — share a genetic similarity distinct from neighboring regions. The Temne, who constitute the largest group in Sierra Leone, call this region home, as do the Mende, who reside across West Africa. In neighboring Côte d'Ivoire and Ghana, the Akan peoples predominate.

Congolese: Beginning around 3,000 years ago, the genetic tapestry of the western Congo basin was transformed by the influx of Bantu- speaking peoples from the highlands of what is today Nigeria and Cameroon. More recently, Bantu speakers in the western Congo region established the historical Kingdom of Kongo, which flourished for over 500 years until its collapse at the hands of colonial powers in 1914. Today, Bantu-speaking peoples (such as the Kongo, Teke, Mbochi, and Sangha) are significant majorities in the countries bordering the Congo River.

Eastern European: Between the eighteenth and twentieth centuries, Eastern Europe was heavily influenced by Imperial (and then Soviet) Russia, but the genetic heritage of Eastern Europe traces back to peoples living southeast of the Baltic Sea as well as to a more recent influx of Slavic- speaking peoples from north of the Black Sea. After the collapse of the Soviet Union in 1991, millions of Eastern Europeans migrated west in search of economic opportunity. In the United States, Eastern European ancestry is most common in the Midwest.

Ethiopian & Eritrean: Despite recent conflict, Eritreans and Ethiopians were united under the powerful Kingdom of Aksum for almost 1,000 years until its collapse in 940 CE, and their DNA reflects that shared history. The region has also served as a crossroads between Africa and the Arabian Peninsula for tens of thousands of years. Today, most Ethiopians and Eritreans have both East African and Arabian ancestry and speak Afro-Asiatic languages, including Oromo, Tigrinya, Arabic, and Amharic.

Filipino & Austronesian: Many indigenous Filipinos, including the Aeta, Batak, and Mamanwa peoples, are likely descended from one of the earliest dispersals of modern humans out of Africa. However, most Filipinos can trace their ancestry to a much more recent and widespread migration of Southeast Asian seafarers related to the indigenous people of Taiwan. Today, this genetic signature – called "Austronesian" (meaning "southern island") – is common across the islands of the Pacific, from the Philippine Sea to Hawaii, and can be found as far away as Madagascar.

Finnish: Finland was peopled by multiple waves of colonization, including a migration of early Uralic peoples from Eastern Europe or western Siberia. Modern Finns are genetically and linguistically distinct from their Nordic and Slavic neighbors, despite centuries of Swedish and then Russian rule. Today, there are up to seven million ethnic Finns worldwide, with over 600,000 living in the United States, concentrated in Minnesota and northwestern Michigan.

French & German: "French and German" people descend from ancient Alpine-Celtic and Germanic populations, and inhabit an area extending from the Netherlands to Austria – roughly corresponding to the extent of Charlemagne's Frankish Kingdom in the Middle Ages. Estimates place Charlemagne himself in the family trees of all modern Europeans, possibly many times over. Genetically and geographically, this population's people are at the heart of Europe.

Iberian: The genetic landscape of the Iberian Peninsula – represented today by the people of Spain and Portugal – was influenced by several Mediterranean civilizations, including 800 years of Arabic North African rule. Now, a small North African genetic signature is present in Iberian DNA, and over eight percent of Spanish words carry Arabic origins. Conquistadors from Portugal and Spain colonized parts of Africa, Oceania, and the Americas, and DNA signatures of Iberian ancestry are now relatively common in people of Latin American descent.

Indonesian, Thai, Khmer & Myanma: From Myanmar to Indonesia, the people of Southeast Asia are genetically diverse, reflecting the legacies of several migrations beginning over 40,000 years ago. More recently, the region has been heavily influenced by Hindu, Buddhist, and Islamic cultures. Before its fall in the fifteenth century, the Khmer empire – encompassing modern-day Thailand, Laos, and Cambodia – was the largest land empire in the region's history.

Italian: Bisected from north to south by the Apennine mountains, the famously boot-shaped Italian peninsula has been home to modern humans for over 30,000 years. In the early Middle Ages, Germanic invaders brought about the fall of the Western Roman Empire, and a northern European genetic signature persists in modern Italians to this day. This influence is strongest in the north, while southern Italians share a rich genetic heritage with Greece.

Japanese: The Japanese Archipelago, composed of a whopping 6,852 islands, was colonized by multiple waves of immigrants beginning as early as 30,000 BCE. Modern Japanese people can trace most of their ancestry to the Stone Age Jōmon and late Stone Age Yayoi cultures. Yayoi DNA is concentrated in the center of Japan, while

Jōmon ancestry persists to the north and south among the culturally distinctive Ainu and Ryukyuan peoples.

Korean: The Korean peninsula was first inhabited by hunter-gatherers who were genetically similar to Stone Age peoples living near the Amur River in eastern Russia. These early Koreans were later joined by Bronze-Age rice farmers from southern China or Vietnam. By the tenth century, Korea was politically and culturally unified and remained so until the establishment of a communist north and a democratic south after the Second World War. Although North and South Koreans are politically divided, they remain genetically similar to one another.

Manchurian & Mongolian: The Manchurian and Mongolian population includes ethnolinguistic minorities like the Daur — who speak a language related to Mongolian — and the Oroqen, who speak a Tungusic language and live near the Amur River basin. These groups reside at the juncture of the Central Asian plains, boreal forests, and the Gobi Desert. Linguistically distinct but genetically similar, Mongolian and Manchurian peoples generally practice shamanism and Tibetan Buddhism.

Native American: The first humans to reach the New World populated much of North, Central, and South America within just a few thousand years following their arrival from northeast Asia around 15,000 years ago. Despite drastic population losses over the past 500 years as a result of exposure to Old World diseases and genocide at the hands of European colonizers, the genetic legacy of these early American trailblazers persists to this day, primarily in Central and South America.

Nigerian: Nigeria's population is the largest in Africa and one of the most diverse, with over 250 ethnic groups. The country's arid north is home to people of mostly Hausa and Fulani descent, while the Yoruba are concentrated in the southwest, the Ijaw in the tropical south, and the Igbo in the southeast. As much as two thirds of African-Americans' Sub-Saharan DNA may trace back to Nigerian ancestors, due to the disproportionate impact of the Atlantic slave trade on the people of the region.

North African & Arabian: Although early humans lived north of the Sahara as early as 300,000 years ago, the recent ancestors of North Africans were more closely related to some non-African populations. This relationship reflects an intricate history of migrations into present-day Morocco, Algeria, Tunisia, Libya, and Egypt from the Arabian Peninsula. An older North African genetic legacy peaks in Berbers of the Maghreb and in the indigenous people of the Canary Islands.

Sardinian: Sardinians are outliers in the genetic landscape of Europe, thanks to the geographic isolation of their rugged island home off of mainland Italy. Over the centuries, Sardinians resisted assimilation by occupying forces and have managed to preserve a few unique traditions, including "Cantu a Tenòre," a haunting style of overtone singing practiced to this day.

Scandinavian: Scandinavians – represented by the people of Norway, Sweden, Denmark, and Iceland – owe much of their linguistic and genetic heritage to North Germanic tribes who established settlements around the North Sea during the late Middle Ages. Many Scandinavians, like the Sámi people in the far north, are descendants of early Scandinavian hunter-gatherers. In the United States, Scandinavian ancestry is most common in North Dakota.

Senegambian & Guinean: The people of Senegal, The Gambia, Guinea, and Guinea-Bissau share many traditions related to the history of powerful empires in the region. In The Gambia, the Mandinka are the largest group, with historical roots along the Niger River basin, while the Wolof form the majority in neighboring Senegal. In Guinea and Guinea-Bissau the Fulani predominate, and may have subtle genetic links to North Africa or Western Asia. Today, around 20% of African American ancestry is from this region.

Siberian: Many ethnolinguistic groups call the northern reaches of Asia home. Among them are the Yukaghir, the Nganasan, and the Turkic- speaking Yakuts, who migrated North and East from southern Siberia between 700-900 years ago to escape encroaching Mongol raiders. Today, the Yakuts are a large ethnic minority in northeastern Siberia and share genetic similarities with other indigenous groups in the region including the Evenks, Evens, and Buryats. Indigenous Siberians are often well adapted to climate extremes, as they face some of the largest annual temperature fluctuations in the world.

Somali: While modern humans have lived in East Africa for over 200,000 years, ethnic Somalis living in Somalia, Eastern Ethiopia and Kenya trace much of their genetic heritage and social structure to 9th century migrations from the Arabian Peninsula. Almost all ethnic Somalis belong to one of five major patrilineal clans and this clan structure is integral to the cultural and political fabric of Somali society. Many Somalis immigrated to North America, Europe, or Western Asia in response to civil war in the twilight of the 20th century.

Southern East African: Within the last 3,000 years, metallurgy and agriculture arrived in Southern East Africa with the migration of Bantu- speaking peoples from the highlands of what is today Nigeria and Cameroon. The historical center of this Eastern Bantu migration lies in the African Great Lakes region that runs along the Western edge of Kenya and Tanzania. Today, the largest ethnic groups in Burundi, Kenya, Rwanda, Tanzania, and Uganda all speak Bantu languages.

Sudanese: Sudan and South Sudan share a distinct genetic heritage dating to early agricultural civilizations, including the Nubian Kingdoms of Kush and Meroë that once flourished along the banks of the upper Nile. Today, the people of Sudan and South Sudan are ethnically diverse, following a long history of intermarriage between indigenous East Africans and migrants from the Arabian peninsula. However, this Arabian genetic legacy is less common in the south of the region.

Unassigned: There is a wide range of human diversity out there, and sometimes our algorithm can't pinpoint a region of your DNA to a specific population. Bear with us as our data and resources continue to expand. We expect the amount of unassigned ancestry our customers see to decrease.

Vietnamese: Present-day Vietnam was the cradle of one of the world's earliest civilizations, and one of the world's first regions to develop rice- based agriculture. A tropical country on the Indochinese Peninsula, Vietnam is bordered by China to the north and by Laos and Cambodia to the west. The country has 54 ethnic groups, the largest being the Kinh, who make up more than 85% of the population.

Western Asian: Domestication of grains and livestock emerged 11,000 years ago in western Asia, sparking the agricultural revolution that eventually spread to Europe, Africa, and the rest of Asia. From the Caucasus to Iran, western Asia is an important crossroads in the human migration out of Africa, and the genetics of this region reflect that role. A western Asian genetic signature also appears in North Africa and southern Europe.

# Cheers to being 100%

# Everett Woolum

Remember, your 23andMe results are a living analysis of your DNA. Visit your reports online, and you may notice more refined results over time.

# GALLERY OF AUTHOR'S PHOTOS

**2006, Everett with Yugoslavian girls**

**2006, Switzerland**

**2006, Yugoslavia, Rosita on Tito's train**

**2007, Trip to Top of Europe**

**2011, Netherlands**

**2013, Ushuaia, Argentina**

**2018- Everett on another adventure, flying over the San Francisco Bay Area**

**2018, Everett at Mary Ann's grave**

**2018, Jesus Burial tomb**

**Adventure on Yantze River - China 2012**

**Black Sea, 2006**

**Brazil 2013**

**Christ the Redeemer, Brazil. 2013**

**Copa Cabana, Brazil 2013**

**China 2012**

**Greece, 2018**

**Heading-out, 2015**

**Norway, 2015**

**Cusco, Peru.   2013**

**Dead Sea - Israel 2018**

**Everett at his home**

**Everett at Parent's gravesite**

## Everett in Santorini, 2018

## Everett retirement ceremony

**Everett with friend, Olivia. Chile, 2013**

**Everett, desk where he wrote his memoir**

## Iguazu Falls, Argentina side, 2013

## Jesus Placed His Hand There -2000 Years Ago

**Kaitlin Woolum, grand-niece, 2020**

**Luxembourg American Military Cemetery, 2007**

**Machu Picchu walls 2013**

**Machu Picchu, Peru  2013**

**Maudie, Christine. Circa 1960**

**Mountains of Olives, Israel. 2018**

**Netherlands, 2007**

**Nova Scotia - Canada, 2019**

**Original Olympic stadium, Greece**

**Picking Chinese Tea Leaves 2012**

**Romania 2006**

**Rosita on Black Sea trip**

**Rosita, Gus, Everett. 2019**

**Samuel Woolum, headstone**

**Sarah Woolum, grand-niece, 2020**

**SSgt Woolum**

**Stake where Apostle Paul was flogged**

**Terra-cotta Soldiers 2012**

**Tiananmen Square 2012**

**Trans-Atlantic cruise 2019, friends Richard and Carolyn Hay**

**Travis AFB, CA**

**Virgil Pauline Christine Everett**

**Virgil, Christine, Pauline, Everett, Circa 1993**

# Wailing Wall - Israel 2018